D1531969

KRISTA O'REILLY-DAVI-DIGUI

About Krista

In the past seven years Krista returned to school, started writing, launched babies into the world as she launched a new business, struggled with fear, anxiety and suicidal thoughts but also learned to ask for help and advocate for her needs.

She walked through surgery, chronic pain, and was diagnosed with an autoimmune disease. She has practiced embracing the truth of what she wants, learned to honor her wiring, and to shore up leaky boundaries. She buried several people she loved, said yes to adventure, worked really hard and gave herself permission to rest. She put down deep, strong roots of self-awareness and self-compassion.

And she picked up joy along the way. Enough to share.

Krista lives in central Alberta, Canada, and works as a writer & Joyful Living Educator. She helps "messy humans" like herself quiet the noise of perfectionism, comparison and fear to show up fully to their imperfect and beautiful lives.

Her message can be summed up in the following simple statements: you're imperfect; life is messy; show up anyway. She'll help you figure out how.

JAIRUS DAVI-DIGUI

All proceeds from the Winter Journal will be used to establish an art scholarship in Jairus' name.

My beautiful son has ended his life after a long, ferocious battle with severe depression and persistent suicidal ideation.

He wanted to live. Wanting to live and knowing how are two different things. And mental illness, just like cancer, is not something we choose. It is not shameful or a reflection of character. And it is not the fullness of who we are.

Jairus was a deep thinker and challenged me to consider and see differently. He was playful, loved to tease, and loved when I'd play video games with him that scared me. (And of course, in no way does this begin to sum up the incredible person he was.) He was also a deeply sensitive soul who wrestled hard. Besides his dad and I, he had a solid crew of friends and his two sisters who also loved him deeply. He knew he was loved.

Jairus knew from the age of 7 or 8 that he wanted to be an illustrator, then animator, and after high school he studied animation and game design. Art was an integral part of who he was – and of our family culture.

I'd like to keep Jairus' name and memory alive in part by helping another young student of his high school art program attend post-secondary studies in the digital or fine arts.

WHY SEASONAL JOURNALING?

It's human to experience ebb and flow in life. We move through seasons of transition and uncertainty; we tilt between self-confidence and self-doubt; we experience shifting levels of energy or productivity and changes in what we need or want.

We witness death and new life.

Life is messy. And beautiful.

Living awake and seasonally allows us to live grateful for the gifts in every season. It means consciously and stubbornly mining for these gifts.

Because there is wisdom knit into the fabric of every season.
Into the light and the dark.

Tuning into the season we're in – both the natural and metaphorical season of life – can help us live gentler, calmer lives.

As we notice patterns and rhythms of mood, energy, creativity, introspection, or cravings, we learn to better tend to our needs and love ourselves with less judgment. We become more attuned to and less fearful or resentful of the ebb and flow of life. We put down deeper, healthy roots of self-awareness and self-compassion that allow us to tilt and flex and not break when the storms come.

And we learn to mine for the achingly beautiful and sometimes heart-wrenchingly challenging gifts inherent in every season.

Krista xo

HOW TO USE THE JOURNAL

52 Mondays: Winter Session is meant to journey with you through 13 weeks of your imperfect and oh, so beautiful life and prompt you to notice what's happening in the natural world around you and in your inner world.

It is an invitation to read one short reflection as you start each fresh, new week and then to ponder or reflect on the practical application to your life as you move through the days ahead.

I have provided 3 journaling or reflection prompts you may choose to use to get your thoughts flowing but they are simply an invitation that you may prefer to leave aside.

I have left the pages undated and unlined as in addition to writing you may choose to doodle or sketch or Washi-Tape in little treasures you find that speak to you of winter.

Finally, at the end of the journal you'll find an opportunity to "rest, replenish, and review" as you consider the greatest lessons you've learned or what you've noticed about life and self in the past 13 weeks. This R&R&R exercise also asks you to identify what you need or want as you step awake and purposeful into winter.

I hope that this simple journal will surprise and delight you. I hope it serves as a gentle yet persistent reminder to tune in to the gifts of this season. And I hope that in even one small way you enter the next season stronger, more self-aware, or happier.

Krista xo

We get to write outselves a new story.

HERE I AM

Here I am - alive but weary and deeply sad - in a season of life that has felt unkind. We didn't have a chance to catch our breath from one challenge or heart-ache before we were hit head-on with more. The impact was fierce.

This is not the story I'd have written for myself.

You might read a chapter or two or think "it could have been worse" or "thank G*d they survived that." And yes, we are so grateful. But if you witness in passing a life ravaged by fire or pain, can you see beyond "it could have been worse?"

Can you also see the emotional devastation, how their life was flipped upside down and shaken violently, how afraid the flesh and bone people inside that life must yet feel?

The story doesn't end with smoldering fire or battered metal or broken hearts. It doesn't end with pulling people to safety, patching them up, or burying one we love. Because bruised hearts and spirits require more than a new dwelling space to feel safe and heard and healed.

But here I am, writing a new story, one faltering line at a time.

Pause & Consider

1. It's tempting to rush through pain to "I'm fine" and "all is well" but I think it's important we also have permission to be raw and real about the reality of our messy lives or harsh experiences.

2. Notice (without judgement) your coping mechanism; what do you use to deal with pain - is it wine, busyness, fits of rage, shopping, tears, hiding under the covers?

3. We get to write ourselves a new story despite the hand we've been dealt. It can feel empowering and healing to remember that no matter what, we can choose to keep writing.

There are gifts to be mined in every season.

You're imperfect. Life is messy. Show up anyway.

There are gifts to be mined in every season.

You're imperfect. Life is messy. Show up anyway.

There are gifts to be mined in every season.

You're imperfect. Life is messy. Show up anyway.

There are gifts to be mined in every season.

You're imperfect. Life is messy. Show up anyway.

What if I dive in heart first.

SMALL MIRACLES

I am not always sure where the time goes
Or how it is that I tessered from there to here
When I was certain tomorrow would never come
And I couldn't imagine life different from where I was.

I'm not always sure how it came to be
That my life, though imperfect, is full of beauty
Though I lost people I love and travailed through storms
Here I stand rooted against all odds in strength, love, and hope.

I'm not at all sure what tomorrow holds
Or if I'll look back and yearn for earlier years
But what if I dive in heart first and open wide
To receive the small miracles of each season in turn.

Pause & Consider

1. At the end of your days, how will you know that you have lived well?

2. Wabi-sabi acknowledges "three simple realities: nothing lasts, nothing is finished, and nothing is perfect." (Wikipedia). How might Wabi Sabi change how you see?

3. I look for "small miracles" every day. I don't think I've ever had a day, no matter how dark, when I couldn't find at least one. Join me?

There are gifts to be mined in every season.

You're imperfect. Life is messy. Show up anyway.

There are gifts to be mined in every season.

You're imperfect. Life is messy. Show up anyway.

There are gifts to be mined in every season.

You're imperfect. Life is messy. Show up anyway.

There are gifts to be mined in every season.

You're imperfect. Life is messy. Show up anyway.

I remember feeling seen and loved.

I REMEMBER

All year my mom stockpiled gifts and inexpensive bobbles and stored them until the rightful day on her closet shelf, along with sweaters and boxes of chocolates. She and her sister made enough baking to supply 10 families. Most years, I think, we still had frozen butter tarts and shortbread in the freezer come February.

But stockings were my favorite part of Christmas.

I'd gingerly pull each item out of the stocking with care, cautious not to lose anything in the mess of paper wrapping, until finally I'd reach down deep into the toe and pull out the thing I loved most. A Christmas ornament to start a little collection of my own.

I don't have much left from her; she's been gone 17 years now. But every year I pull out my small box of eclectic ornaments and I remember.

I remember feeling seen and loved. I remember mattering. I remember friendship.

She helped me start the collection for our first born too and I've continued on ever since. And one day I hope, long after I'm gone, my children will pull out their own special boxes and remember.

Pause & Consider

1. If your family had any special holidays or traditions, how did they make you feel?

2. Are there a couple traditions you'd like to bring into your life or family? Why do they matter?

3. Perhaps you've carried around unhealthy traditions and are ready to release them. Name them and let them go. Share them with a trusted accountability partner if that feels helpful.

There are gifts to be mined in every season.

You're imperfect. Life is messy. Show up anyway.

There are gifts to be mined in every season.

You're imperfect. Life is messy. Show up anyway.

There are gifts to be mined in every season.

You're imperfect. Life is messy. Show up anyway.

There are gifts to be mined in every season.

You're imperfect. Life is messy. Show up anyway.

Ordinary life is magical too.

ORDINARY MAGIC

The streets are black apart from the meager light cast by the streetlamps. But this is more than enough light to illuminate the sparkle of the snowflakes as they begin to winter.

You sense magic in the air.

You throw on a tuque and warm mitts, lace up fuzzy boots, and head out for an impromptu night-time stroll. You can see your breath and small droplets of ice form on the thick scarf wrapped tightly around your neck.

And in this moment, you experience a deep peace. It will only take a half hour or so for the streets to appear as though they are being washed clean by a crunchy layer of white and it feels like maybe your spirit is being washed clean too.

The world is hushed and as you walk through the neighborhood you catch glimpses of people through windows, watching TV or preparing a meal to share, and you witness from the outside that ordinary life is magical too. It is no small thing.

The snow melts quickly as it hits your coat and your fingers become stiff with cold. "One more block," you think, unwilling to rush away this brief moment in time.

Pause & Consider

1. I think magic comes in the ordinary - for those willing to see. Do you want more space or permission in your life to pause and notice?

2. What are a few practical or concrete things you can do that will allow you to embrace this season more fully?

3. Time in nature in every season can feel restorative; do you want to get out more or perhaps bring a little more nature closer to home?

There are gifts to be mined in every season.

You're imperfect. Life is messy. Show up anyway.

There are gifts to be mined in every season.

You're imperfect. Life is messy. Show up anyway.

There are gifts to be mined in every season.

You're imperfect. Life is messy. Show up anyway.

There are gifts to be mined in every season.

You're imperfect. Life is messy. Show up anyway.

Becoming

ON LEARNING TO USE OUR VOICE

As I learn to move from head to heart into greater vulnerability
there is a risk that I will say or do the wrong thing.
In setting boundaries or expressing what I want and need
I notice the potential for making others uncomfortable or even hurt.
But I see no way to step into deeper freedom and compassion
and also avoid all discomfort.
I take responsibility for my own feelings - for who and how I want to be
and trust others to do their own work too.
Because if I hide from this, from this important work,
then I move away from the people I care most about
instead of moving toward.
In moving toward there is always risk.
And we can hold space for ourselves and for each other
as we do this work of becoming.
Of vulnerability.
And of offering kindness to both self and others as we walk gently,
hand on heart.

Pause & Consider

*1. Which of your brains do you tend to lead with - the head, the heart, or the gut?
Which feels the weakest or hardest to access?*

2. What are you unwilling to feel?

*3. Going deeper in our relationships necessitates vulnerability (heart work) but not
everyone is willing or resourced to do so. Is there a relationship in your life that you
realize cannot go deeper in this season? Will you walk away or can you simply meet the
person where they're at?*

There are gifts to be mined in every season.

You're imperfect. Life is messy. Show up anyway.

There are gifts to be mined in every season.

You're imperfect. Life is messy. Show up anyway.

There are gifts to be mined in every season.

You're imperfect. Life is messy. Show up anyway.

There are gifts to be mined in every season.

You're imperfect. Life is messy. Show up anyway.

A little bit out of the mold.

BEAUTY IN IMPERFECTION

I have always loved moose.

I see them as an intriguing example of beauty in imperfection. They're a bit gangly with awkward angles. Stunning and exuding a powerful presence but also a tiny bit off-beat.

They are full of character yet reminiscent of a wise elder. Like someone who has walked through the fire but has not lost their ability to laugh heartily.

An intriguing tangle of gentle pride and authority, integrity and innate wisdom without the need to assert dominance. Generally calm but not to be trifled with.

Moose are not of a "conventional beauty" like the luscious and powerful kapha presence of a bear, say, or the sleek and quick pitta energy of a mountain lion. I see myself mirrored in the stable pitta-kapha presence of the moose.

And perhaps it's precisely because of their "imperfections" that moose draw me in. How they seem a little bit out of the mold. And how they remind me that beauty really isn't just about the exterior stuff, that we each have an important place in this world, but also that we don't have to take life quite so seriously as I'm wont to do.

Pause & Consider

1. I'm only a dabbler in Ayurveda - do you know your dominant mind-body type or dosha?

2. Is there a particular animal that you love and which speaks to wisdom to you?

3. It feels like life is a daily invitation to "practice what we preach." I preach beauty in imperfection and purpose & joy in every season. How about you?

There are gifts to be mined in every season.

You're imperfect. Life is messy. Show up anyway.

There are gifts to be mined in every season.

You're imperfect. Life is messy. Show up anyway.

There are gifts to be mined in every season.

You're imperfect. Life is messy. Show up anyway.

There are gifts to be mined in every season.

You're imperfect. Life is messy. Show up anyway.

I have what it takes.

ON CHOOSING TO FORGIVE

I decided this morning to forgive. This past year it felt like life was happening TO me. I was doing my best and other people kept causing harm or not doing their jobs or making mistakes that cost money, health, energy, and even a life.

I realized this morning that I have a hard choice to make - I can drown in hate and pain or I can forgive.

I see that my life is really on loan, and everything I consider mine is also simply on loan. Stuff doesn't make or destroy a purposeful life. Injustice can only break me if I agree. Sorrow and suffering can only drown me if I believe the story that I am a victim and that I don't have what it takes.

But I do. I have what it takes.

We may as well admit that life can be crushing; false positivity does not heal. Sometimes we need ample time and support to find wholeness again and it can be a long, uncomfortable process.

But let's also witness that we are still here *choosing* to find our way forward.

And messy or not, for my survival I've decided on the path of forgiveness.

Pause & Consider

1. Is there a need in your life for forgiveness, for self or others, in order to find your way forward?

2. We may rail and argue with reality but there is no healing or momentum in this choice. Though not easy, accepting what is makes room for us to show up fully to the life in front of us.

3. Is it possible that you are far stronger and more capable than you've given yourself credit for?

There are gifts to be mined in every season.

You're imperfect. Life is messy. Show up anyway.

There are gifts to be mined in every season.

You're imperfect. Life is messy. Show up anyway.

There are gifts to be mined in every season.

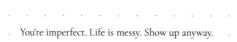
You're imperfect. Life is messy. Show up anyway.

There are gifts to be mined in every season.

You're imperfect. Life is messy. Show up anyway.

Winter invites us to trust.

SYMMETRY

Contrasting with the earthy new promise of spring, lushness of summer, and vibrant cacophony of winter, winter quietly reminds us of the transience of things.

Life wants to be enjoyed in the moment, or in season, lest we miss out altogether.

In winter we witness the authentic beauty of the world. Stripped of most color, sheen, and easy comfort, she is laid bare and unpretentious. Matter of fact.

We see the truth that endings and waiting, seasons of hardship or being hidden, are as natural as new life, productivity, and celebration. And nothing lasts forever.

We cling desperately to what we know, to the gifts of yesteryear, to who we were, but eventually all things must pass away or change and evolve. Winter invites us to trust.

In acceptance we find we are rooted. In coming face to face with the reality of what is we become reacquainted with our truest selves.

We are part of the morning tide, the double rainbow, the geese flying in formation, the Chinook winds. We are part of the circle of life and all of it is impermanent. Yet this does not diminish the breath-catching beauty, poetry,

Pause & Consider

1. What do you hope to leave behind when it is your time to pass from this world?

2. If you are in a season of waiting or being hidden, what is it you long or hope for?

3. What do you notice in your body, heart, or thoughts when you consider the evanescence of life? Is there a message here for you?

There are gifts to be mined in every season.

You're imperfect. Life is messy. Show up anyway.

There are gifts to be mined in every season.

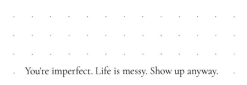
You're imperfect. Life is messy. Show up anyway.

There are gifts to be mined in every season.

You're imperfect. Life is messy. Show up anyway.

There are gifts to be mined in every season.

You're imperfect. Life is messy. Show up anyway.

*Hope lights the path for us
even in the darkest seasons.*

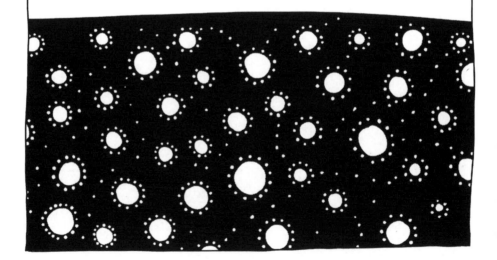

ALMOST BUT NOT QUITE

You know that feeling at the end of winter when the world begins to melt and the blanket of darkness lifts a little at the corner? The days finally begin to lengthen and you can hardly contain your optimism.

You shouldn't get your hopes up too high just yet; you've been tricked many a year before. Just when you store away the mitts and toques, the day after you've returned winter coats and boots to storage, it snows again.

Mother nature chuckles as she kicks up fresh powder and dumps you back into another week of deep freeze. The birds fluff themselves up proud against the bitter chill and you put out a little extra seed in solidarity.

It's just around the bend now - close enough that you can almost smell the wet spring earth. But you're so impatient in the meantime. Deeply uncomfortable in the waiting.

Like when after nine months, heavy and swollen, you await your unborn babe's arrival to the world but he's playing hard to get.

Or when you come to the end of yourself and wearily loosen your grip, ready and longing for different or other.

Almost but not quite.

Pause & Consider

1. I love the reminder that we've already survived 100% of our hard days (because here we are!). Do you need this reminder?

2. Waiting can be hard and teach us plenty about our character. Who are you when asked to wait?

3. I love the Emily Dickenson poem Hope is the Thing With Feathers. Hope lights the path for us even in the darkest seasons. What is your relationship with hope?

There are gifts to be mined in every season.

You're imperfect. Life is messy. Show up anyway.

There are gifts to be mined in every season.

You're imperfect. Life is messy. Show up anyway.

There are gifts to be mined in every season.

You're imperfect. Life is messy. Show up anyway.

There are gifts to be mined in every season.

You're imperfect. Life is messy. Show up anyway.

I want you to simply walk with me.

WALK WITH ME

I don't want you to say there is purpose in my pain.

I don't want you to say that it will get easier over time.

I don't want you to tell me to just pray more because all the words I have are filled with rage.

I want you to sit with me.

I don't want you to fish for details that aren't yours to hear.

I don't want you to tell me how I ought to be or heal.

I don't want your advice or hopeful assurances because the reality is you have no idea.

I want you to hear me.

I don't want your judgement or your shame.

I don't want you to say you know how I feel.

I don't want to live with false positivity to make you comfortable because both pain and joy have their place.

I want you to simply walk with me.

Pause & Consider

1. There can be pressure in our society to live with a false and relentless positivity but spiritual bypassing does not lead to true healing or reparation. You don't have to always be OK.

2. Are you practiced at setting intentional boundaries and communicating them in healthy ways?

3. Are you a good listener? It's so tempting to jump in with advice, our own experiences, or even judgement. But listening is one of the most prized gifts we can offer each other.

There are gifts to be mined in every season.

You're imperfect. Life is messy. Show up anyway.

There are gifts to be mined in every season.

You're imperfect. Life is messy. Show up anyway.

There are gifts to be mined in every season.

You're imperfect. Life is messy. Show up anyway.

There are gifts to be mined in every season.

You're imperfect. Life is messy. Show up anyway.

In time I find my way back to happy.

HAPPY

I pause and notice how breath fills up my lungs and feel the sunlight that filters through the craggy tree outside and through the window to touch me lightly on my cheek. I am happy.

I hug my child and laugh with her and choose to be here, fully present in this precious moment. I pull my thoughts back from all that is unresolved in life or where I feel behind. And I feel happy.

I still myself to really taste my hot coffee with the perfect amount of foam, to look up from my laptop and delight in the contrast of vivid white snow against the spotted birch and evergreens. I am allowed to be happy.

I notice all the things I'm doing well instead of only where I struggle and practice seeing that everyone else is doing their best too; I release my grip on needing life to be perfect. I make space to be happy.

I allow myself to feel - anxiety, rage, resentment, grief, peace, surrender, joy - and remember this is what it means to be human and nothing is permanent. I ground myself and breathe through it. In time I find my way back to happy.

Pause & Consider

1. What do you think about the idea that instead of chasing happiness we could simply choose to BE happy?

2. 15-20% of the population are thought to be "highly sensitive" or HSP's. There are many gifts inherent in this trait and also challenges like not always knowing how to process the depth and weight of emotion you experience.

3. Sometimes there are no words. Only presence, or choosing to just be here in this one small moment in time.

There are gifts to be mined in every season.

You're imperfect. Life is messy. Show up anyway.

There are gifts to be mined in every season.

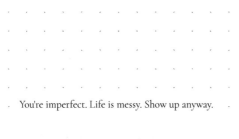
You're imperfect. Life is messy. Show up anyway.

There are gifts to be mined in every season.

You're imperfect. Life is messy. Show up anyway.

There are gifts to be mined in every season.

You're imperfect. Life is messy. Show up anyway.

Winter cannot last forever.

WINTER

There are seasons of life that take your breath away. That make you wonder if you'll ever remember how to breathe normally again.

Seasons in which the loneliness or ache is so deep and profound it could swallow you whole and you don't have the energy to do much more than tread water. Even that is asking a lot.

Still you get out of bed and drink water and put on the kettle. You hug your children and pay bills and remember to eat once in a while. It feels like play-acting but you keep moving.

It feels wrong that everyone else's lives keep spinning, that people laugh and banter easily. Their life has not been splintered. Fractured into a million icy shards.

Life will never be the same again. It can't be.

But no matter the tales your brain and heart spin, Spring always comes again.

Ice thaws and warmer winds begin to blow. One day you'll notice yourself smiling or catch a quick glimmer of light and hope. It's not that all will be well or that you'll ever forget. But for now, all you have to do is hunker down and wait.

Winter cannot last forever.

Pause & Consider

1. When life feels deeply hard, small rhythms/routines keep me living. I refer to this as my "back to basics list." What handful of small routines or practices can help you keep moving forward?

2. Do you need support in this season? Please remember that there is zero shame in needing support or in simply being a real human in a messy world.

3. Mother Teresa said "If we have no peace, it is because we have forgotten that we belong to each other." We don't have to do life alone - we don't have to be perfect to belong and to matter.

There are gifts to be mined in every season.

You're imperfect. Life is messy. Show up anyway.

There are gifts to be mined in every season.

You're imperfect. Life is messy. Show up anyway.

There are gifts to be mined in every season.

You're imperfect. Life is messy. Show up anyway.

There are gifts to be mined in every season.

You're imperfect. Life is messy. Show up anyway.

Some memories are forever.

BUILDING A LIFE

When I was little, my dad took my sisters and I skidooing. We'd bundle up warmly and he'd pull us on a wooden sleigh behind the used Ski-Doo that always smelled of gasoline. We'd tumble off in turn despite holding on for dear life. He'd circle back or we'd trudge through the snow to catch up.

Eventually we'd get too cold so he'd unzip the top of his snowsuit, pull off our sticky mittens, and warm our small icy hands under his armpits like only a dad knows how to do.

Then we'd all head back to his office for a packet of hot chocolate with mini-marshmallows.

Some memories are forever.

It's easy to dismiss the ordinariness of life: game nights and favorite desserts, bedtime stories and bubble baths, or walking to the corner store for frosty slurpees after a sticky soccer match.

We may feel our lives are not enough. Perhaps we wish we'd have had more money or opportunity to offer our kids when they were little. But back rubs and dancing in the kitchen, playing video games together or laughing around a humble meal - these simple moments matter.

This is how we build a life.

Pause & Consider

1. The Danish concept of Hygge can help us enjoy winter by consciously creating a feeling of cosiness, comfort, contentment, and community in our homes. What are a few small ways you can bring hygge into your life or home?

2. Do you notice feeling like your life is not enough? This is often rooted in false comparisons or living in the (imaginary) future. You get to determine what enough looks, feels, and sounds like.

3. Are you walking out your primary values in your day to day life?

There are gifts to be mined in every season.

You're imperfect. Life is messy. Show up anyway.

There are gifts to be mined in every season.

You're imperfect. Life is messy. Show up anyway.

There are gifts to be mined in every season.

You're imperfect. Life is messy. Show up anyway.

There are gifts to be mined in every season.

You're imperfect. Life is messy. Show up anyway.

Rest

Replenish

Review

Consider the greatest lessons you've gleaned about life or self in the past 13 weeks.

Where do you notice yourself struggling or meeting with ongoing resistance?

You're imperfect. Life is messy. Show up anyway.

Consider the greatest lessons you've gleaned
about life or self in the past 13 weeks.

Identify what you've done well at and where you're proud
of yourself for how you've show up to life.

There are gifts to be mined in every season.

*Consider the greatest lessons you've gleaned
about life or self in the past 13 weeks.*

What do you most need or want as you step awake and purposeful
into the next season of life?

You're imperfect. Life is messy. Show up anyway.

BETSY HUGGINS

About Betsy

Krista has been my coach and cheerleader for over a year now. I found her at a time when I was searching for answers, and her words spoke to me in a very meaningful way. Through her incredible understanding of the human spirit I have started to recognise, and respect my own natural strengths and struggles.

I am not a writer, yet through Krista's writing I have learnt what it means to communicate. We all have thoughts and stories we use to make sense of the world, but we all also have our own ways of expressing these thoughts.
Mine is a messy mixture of making things, with lines and with pixels. Krista's words light a spark in my soul that inspires me to try to make sense of my own stories in a creative way.

These doodles you see in this journal are those. Expressions of thoughts and feelings that have been inspired by Krista's words. Simple, and honest. I hope Krista's words, and possibly my drawings, inspire you to go on your own journey inside, as I believe the gifts you will uncover are priceless.

With love,
Betsy x

If you want to say hello, I'd like that, I'm on Instagram @tinygiantlife

Made in the USA
Middletown, DE
30 November 2019